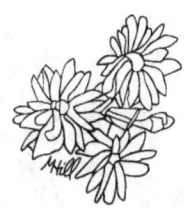

ISBN-13: 978-1717325389
ISBN-10: 1717335386

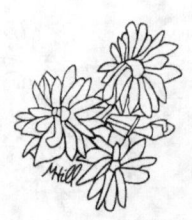

Flowers for Coloring

a Coloring Book of Artful Joy
for Healing and Relaxation

Artwork
by
Marjie Hill

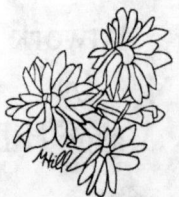

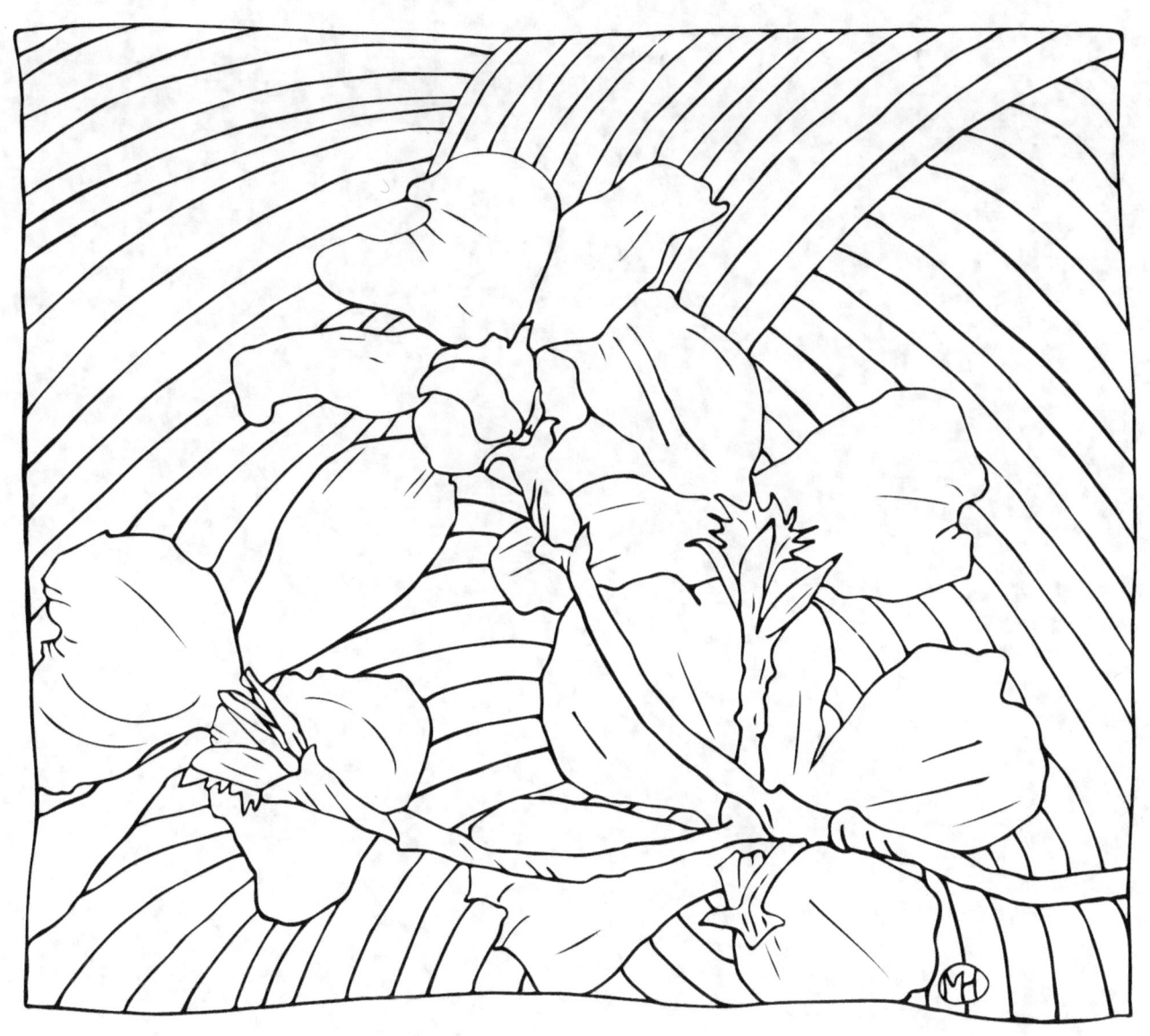

*All things were made through him, and without him
was not anything made that was made.*

John 1:3

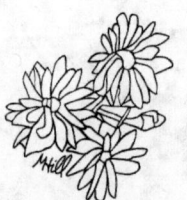

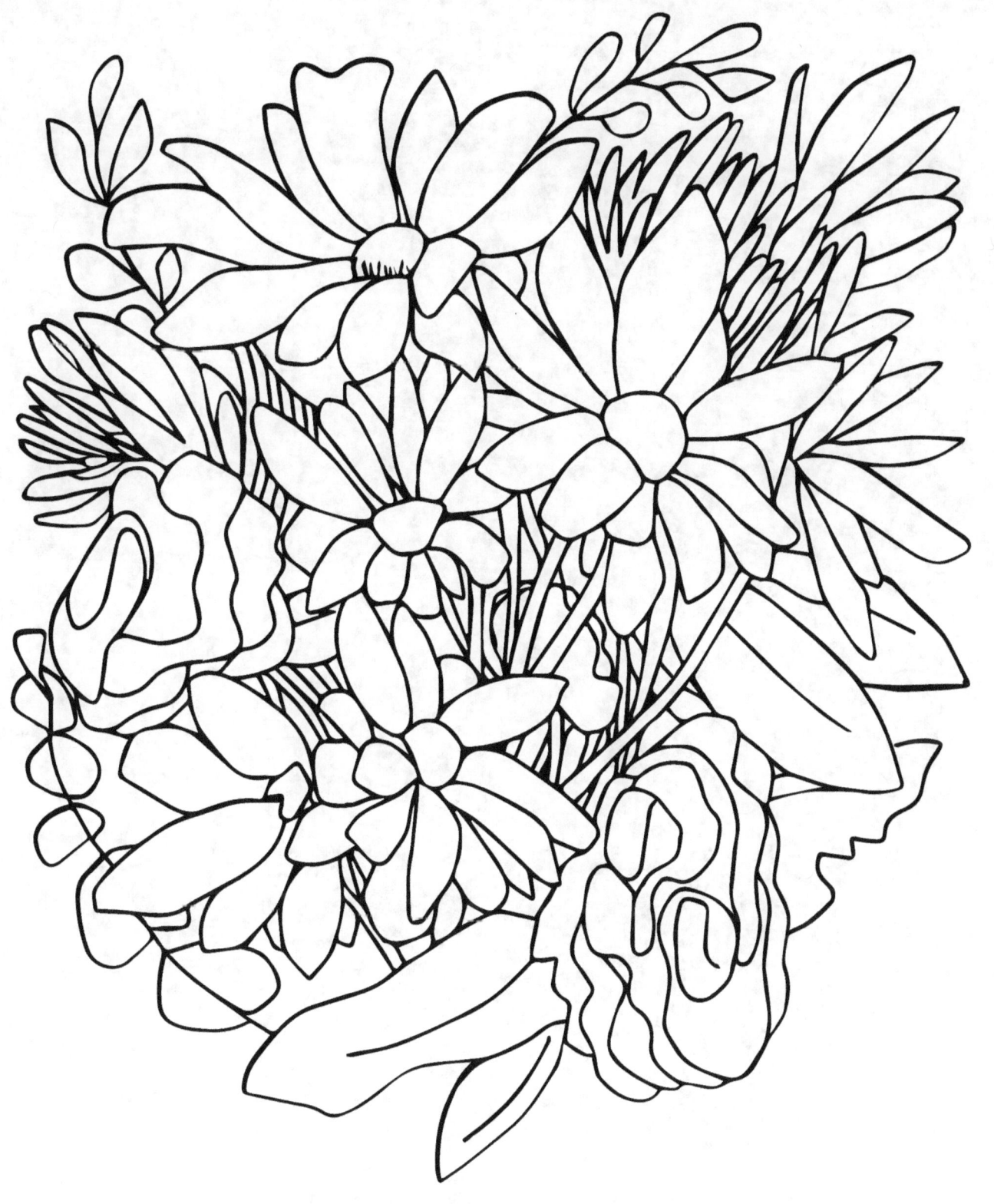

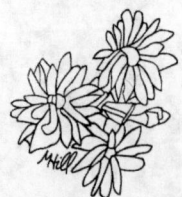

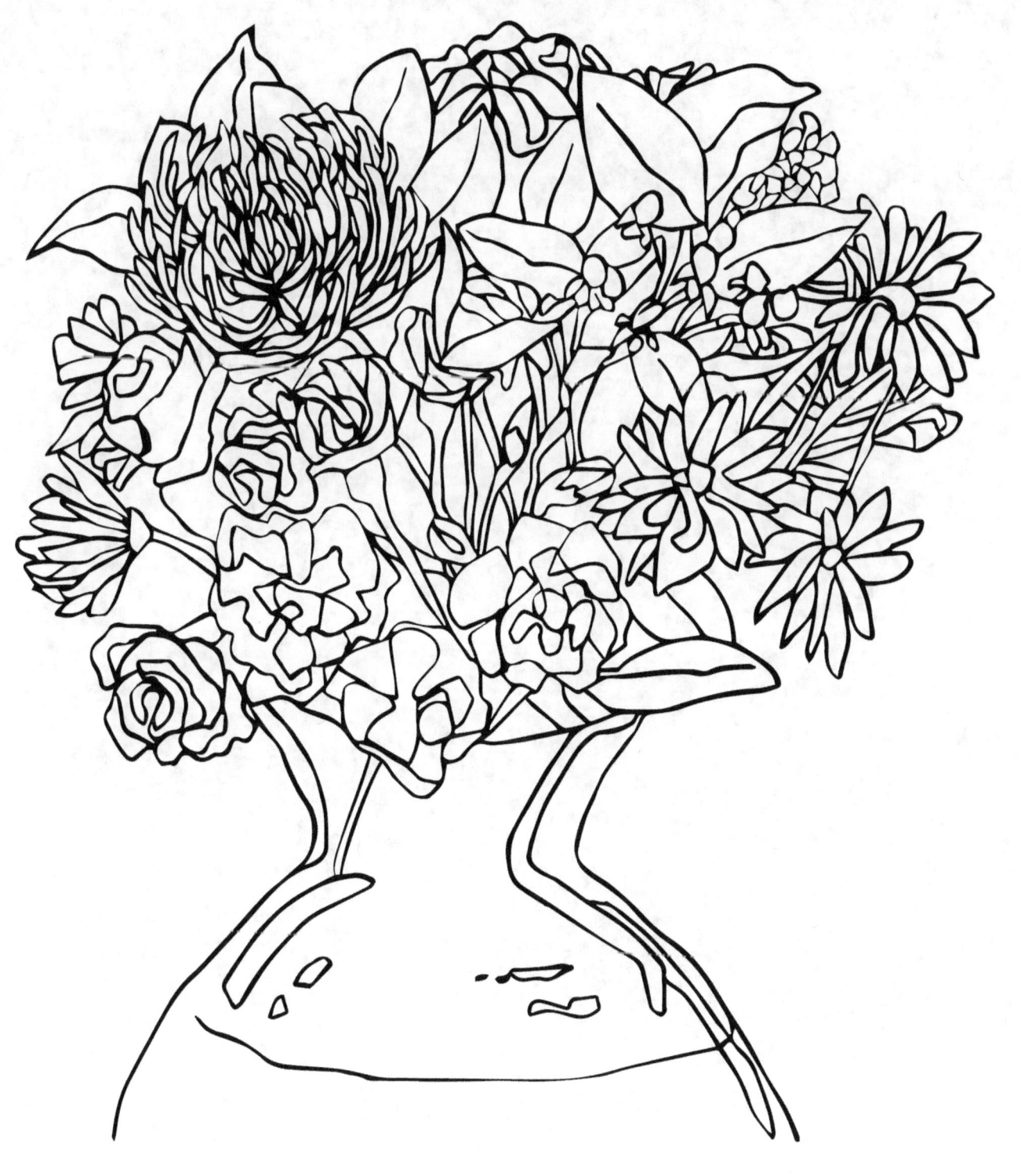

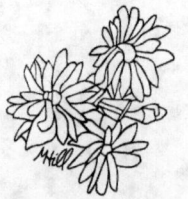

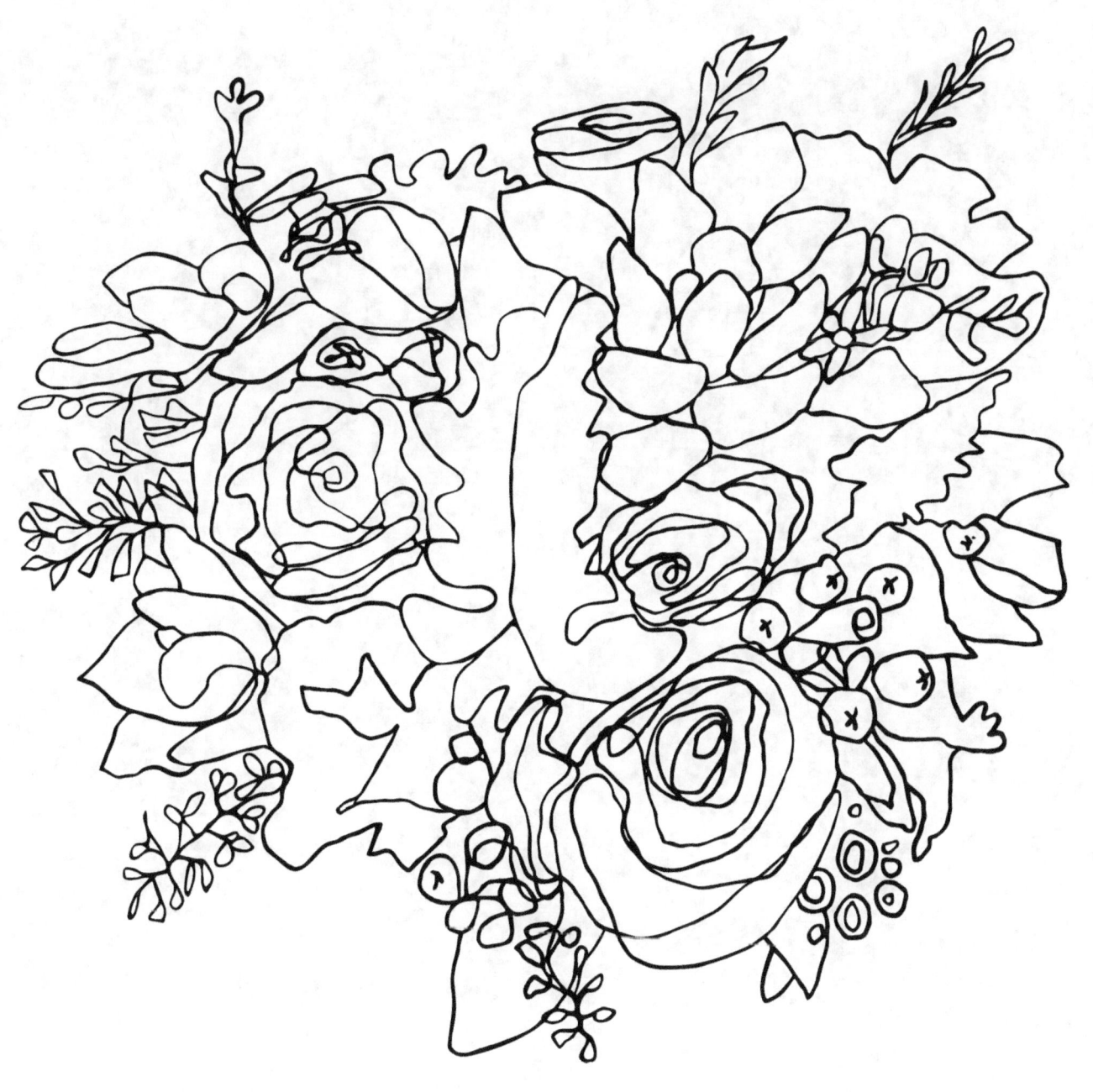

..blow on my garden, that it's fragrance may spread everywhere...

Song of Solomon 4:16

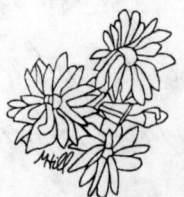

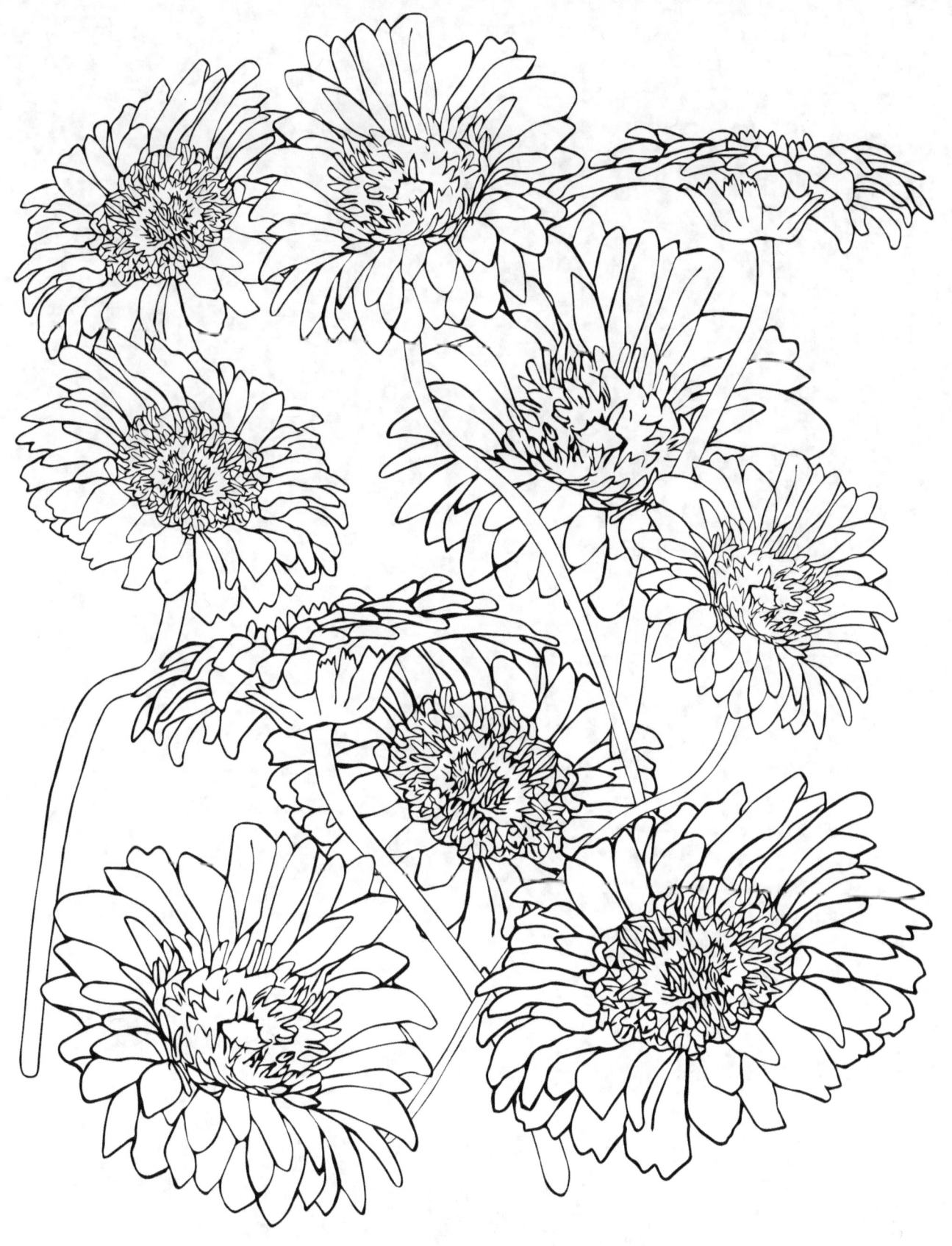

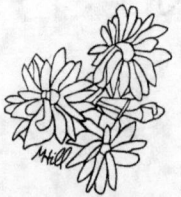

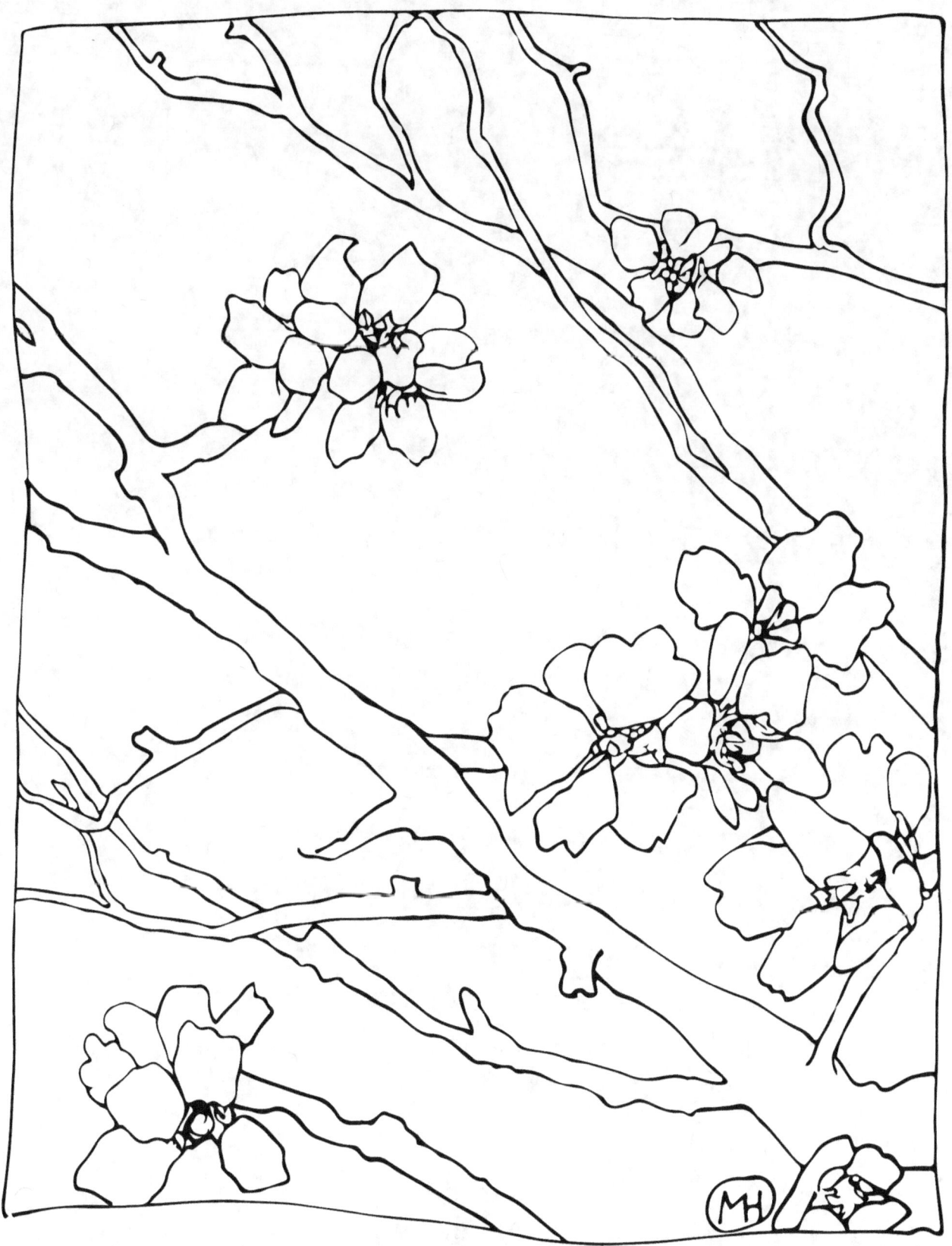

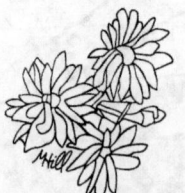

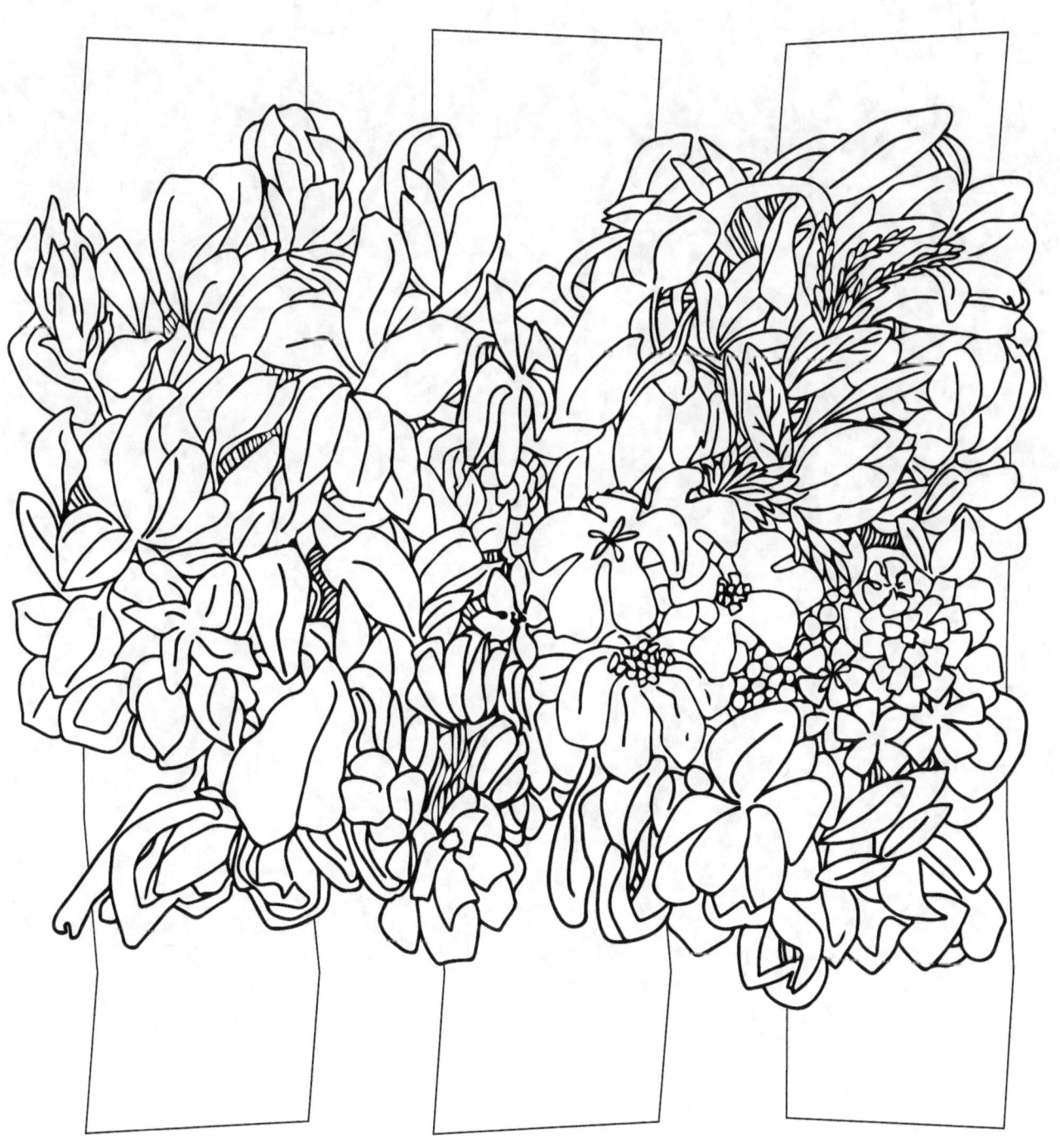

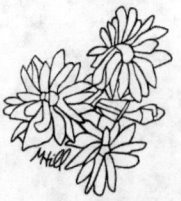

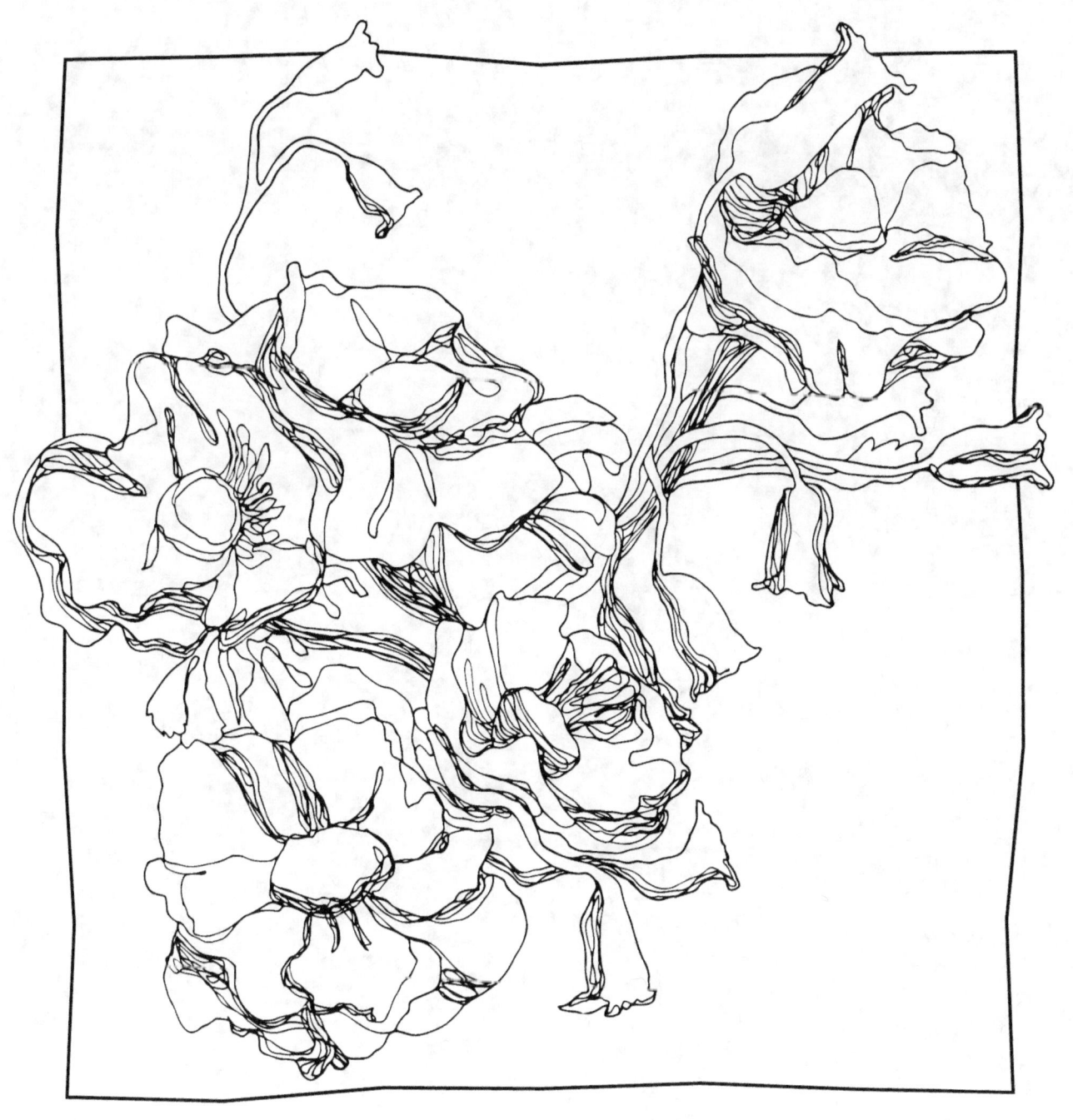

For everything there is a season, and a time
for every matter under heaven...
Ecclesiastes 3:1

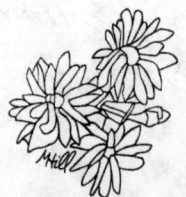

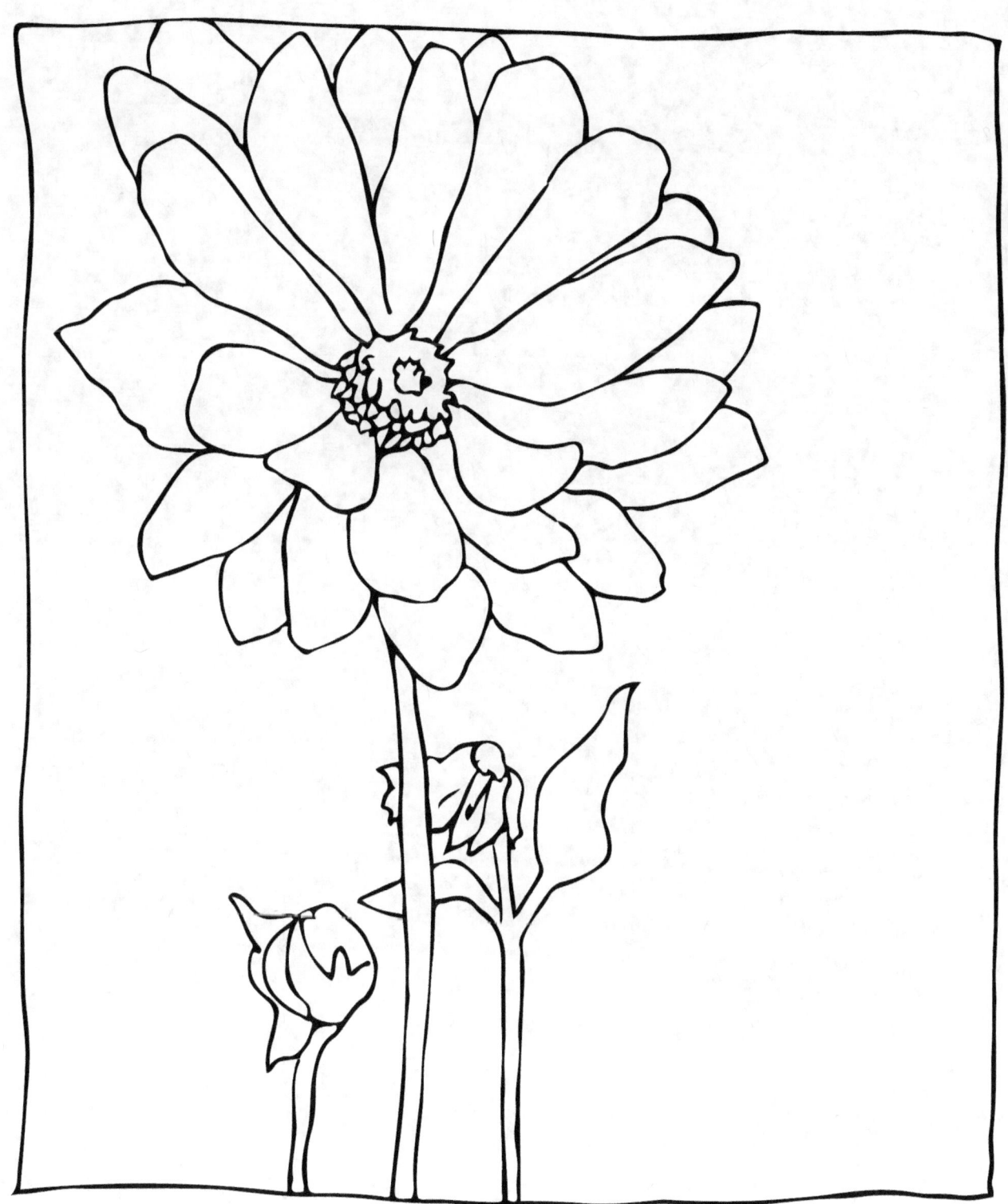

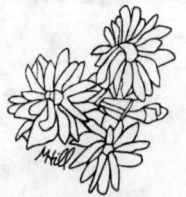

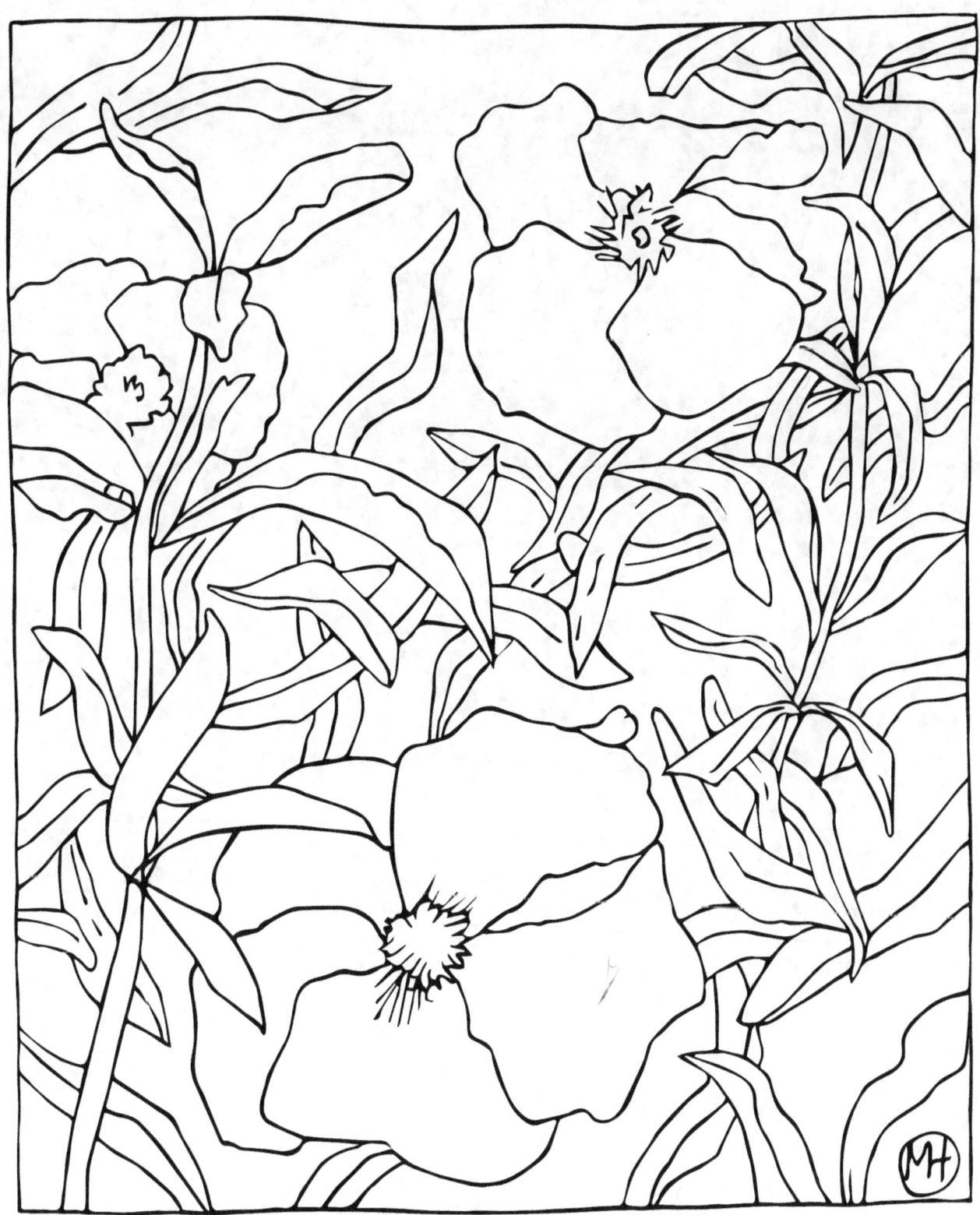

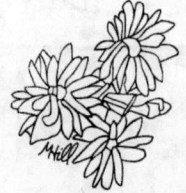

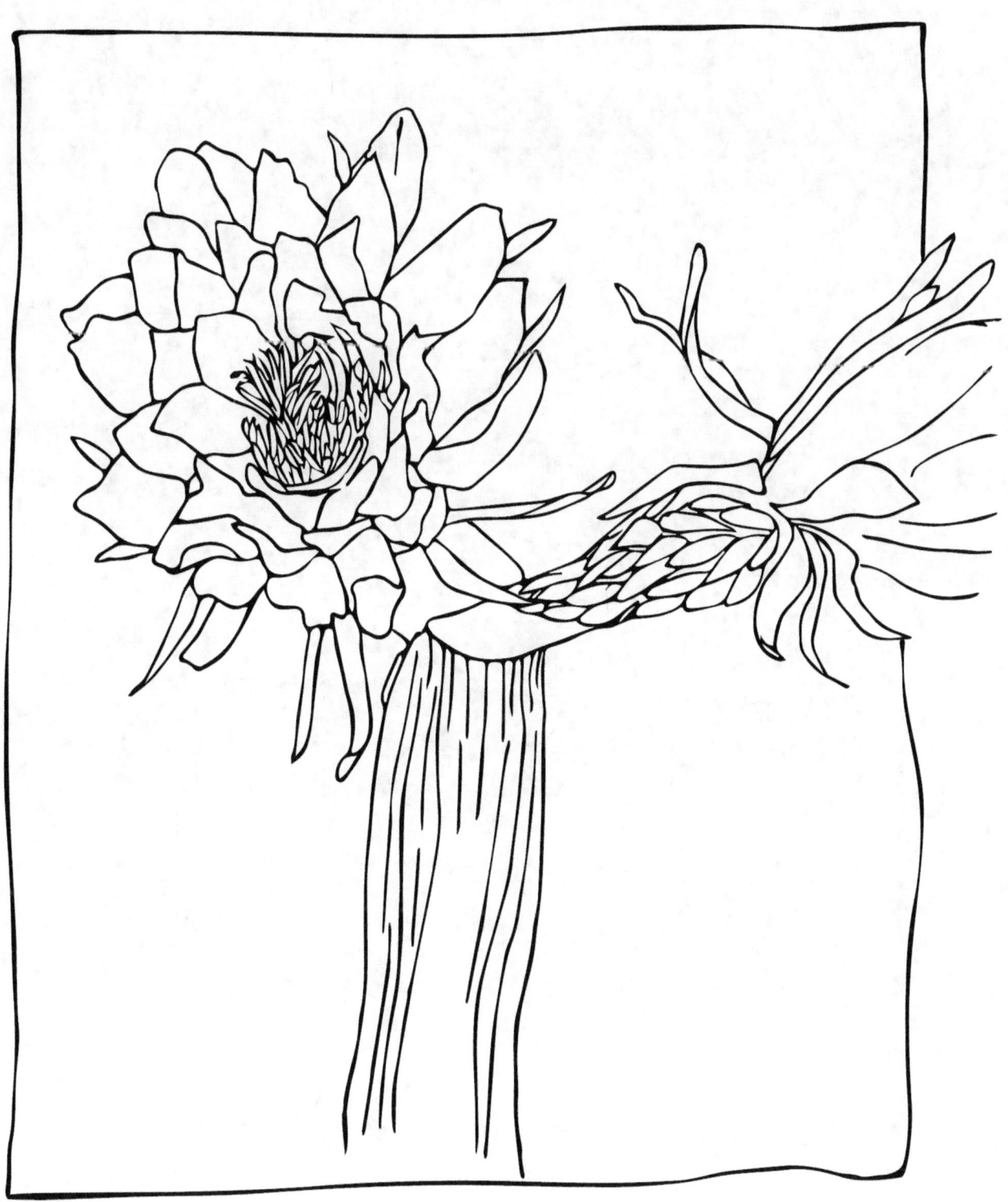

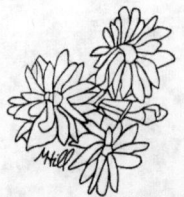

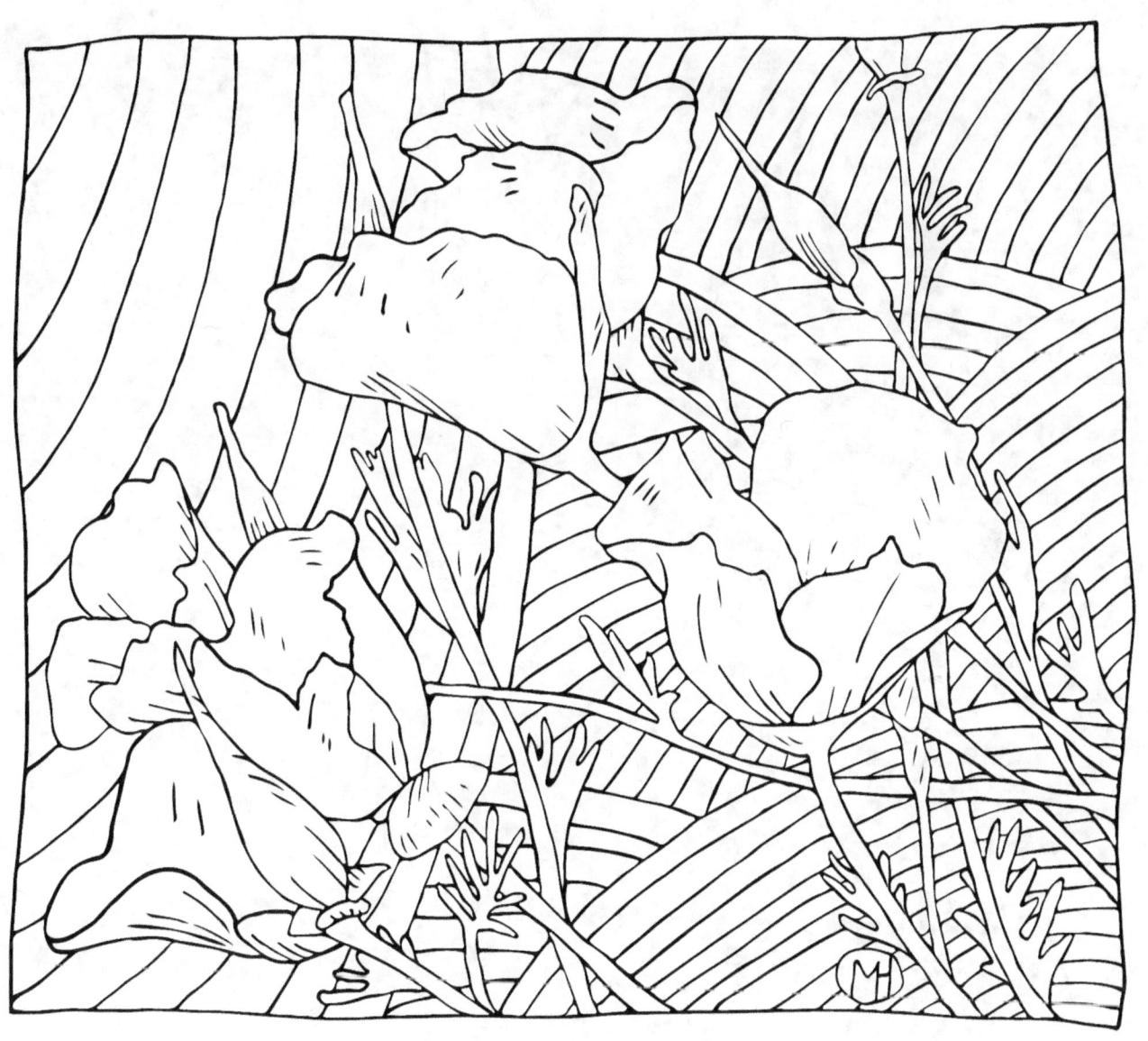

Consider how the wildflowers grow...
Luke 12:27

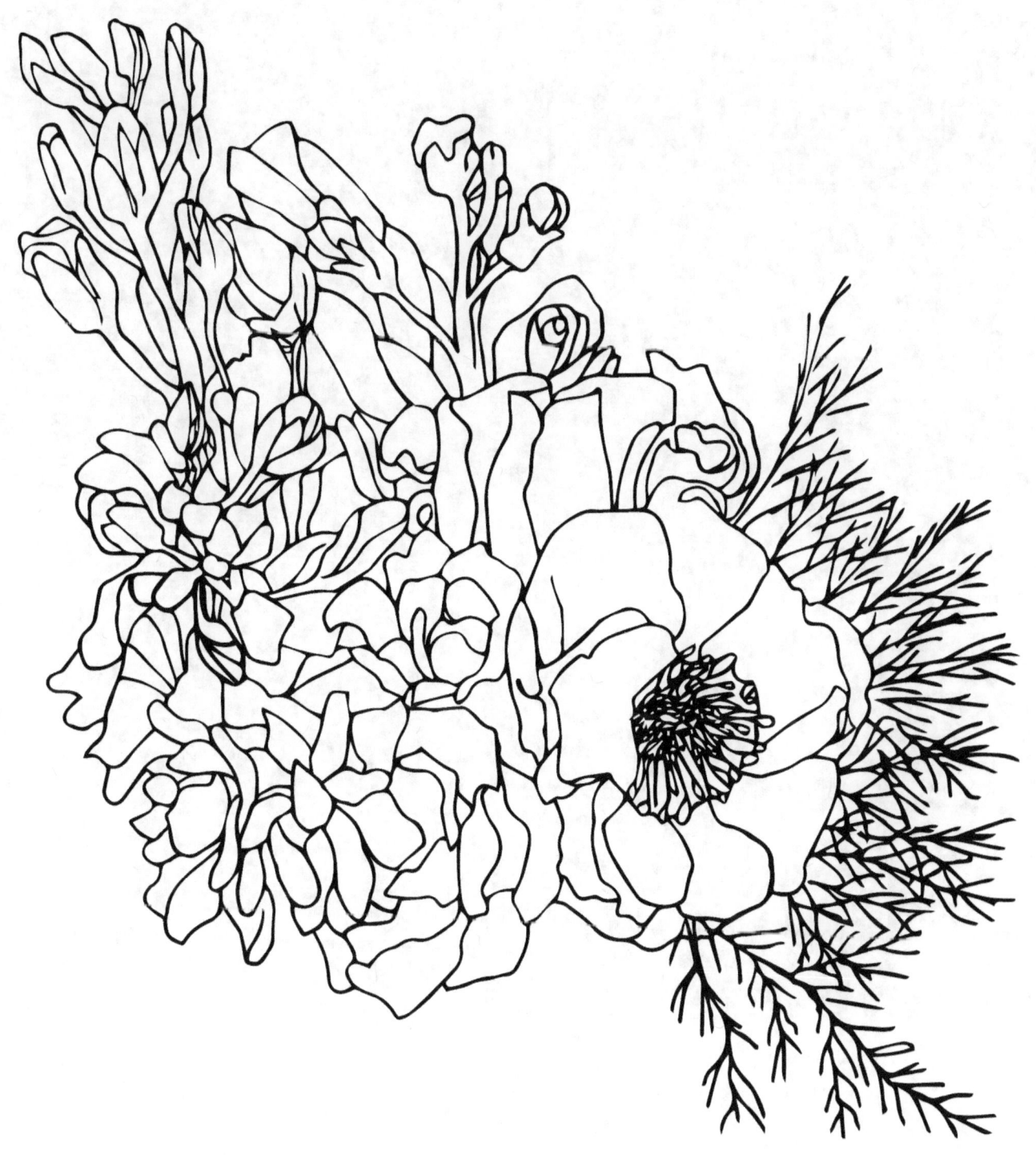

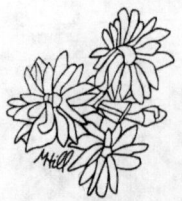

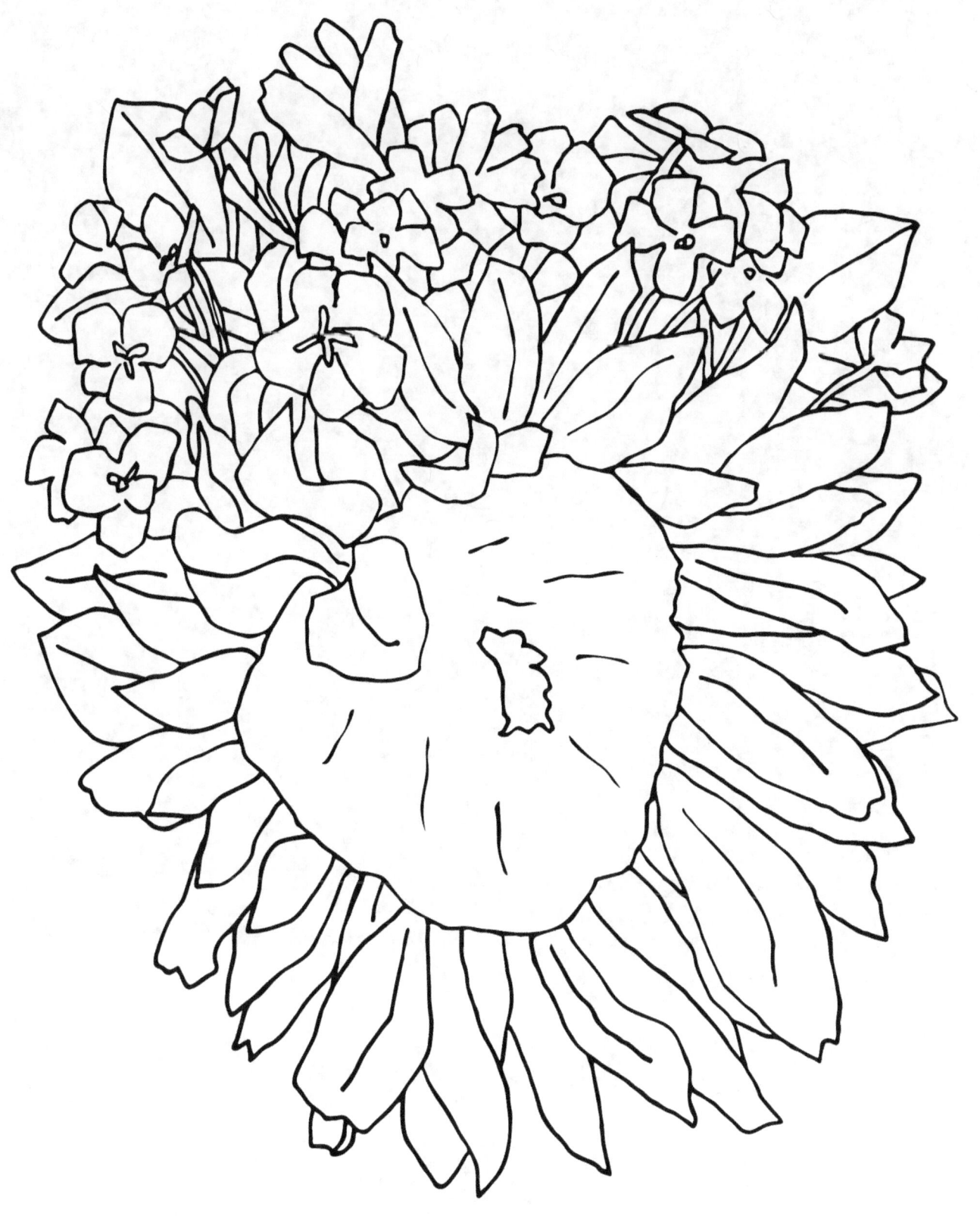

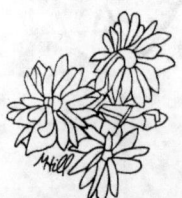

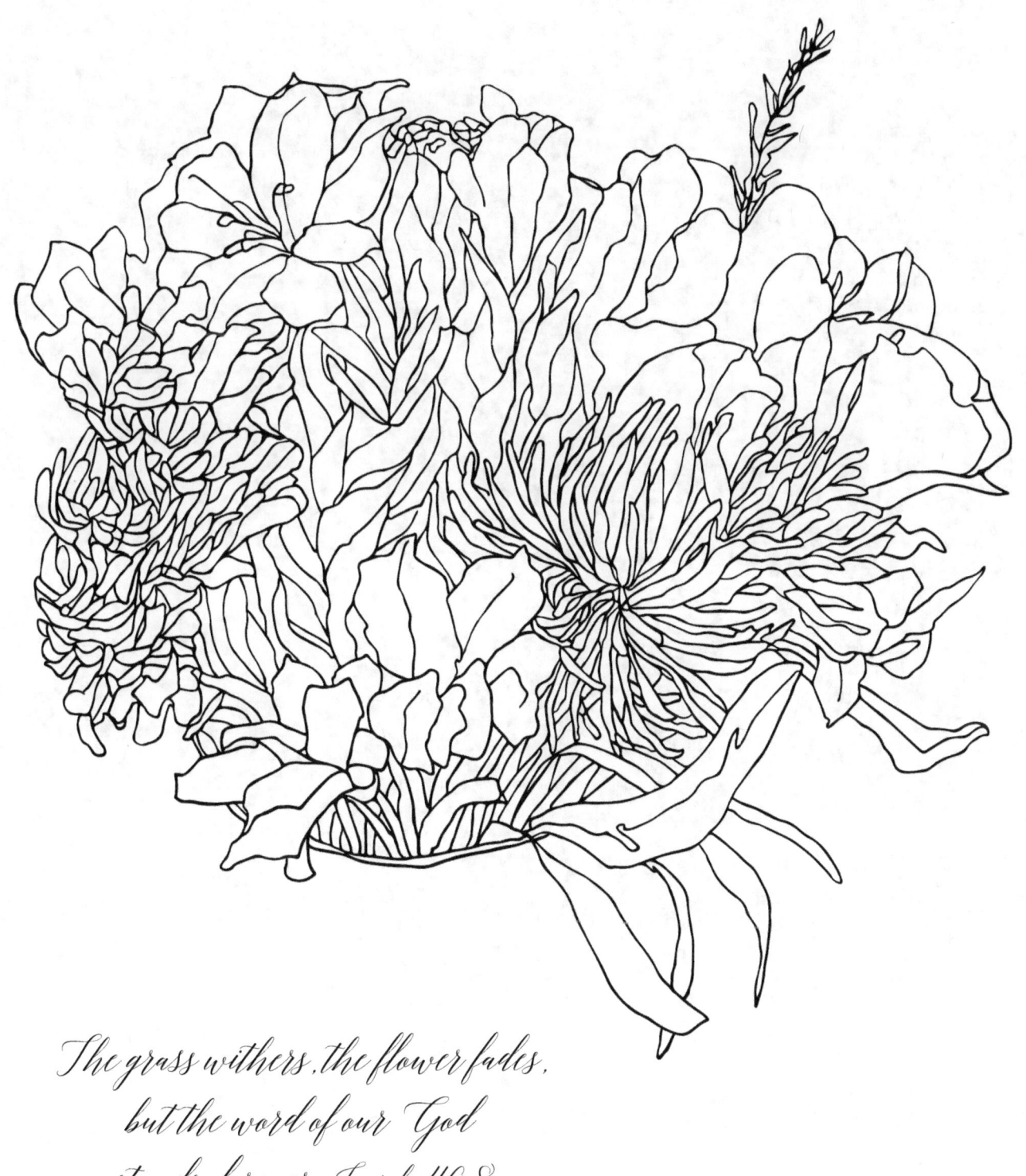

The grass withers, the flower fades,
but the word of our God
stands forever. Isaiah 40:8

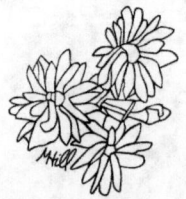

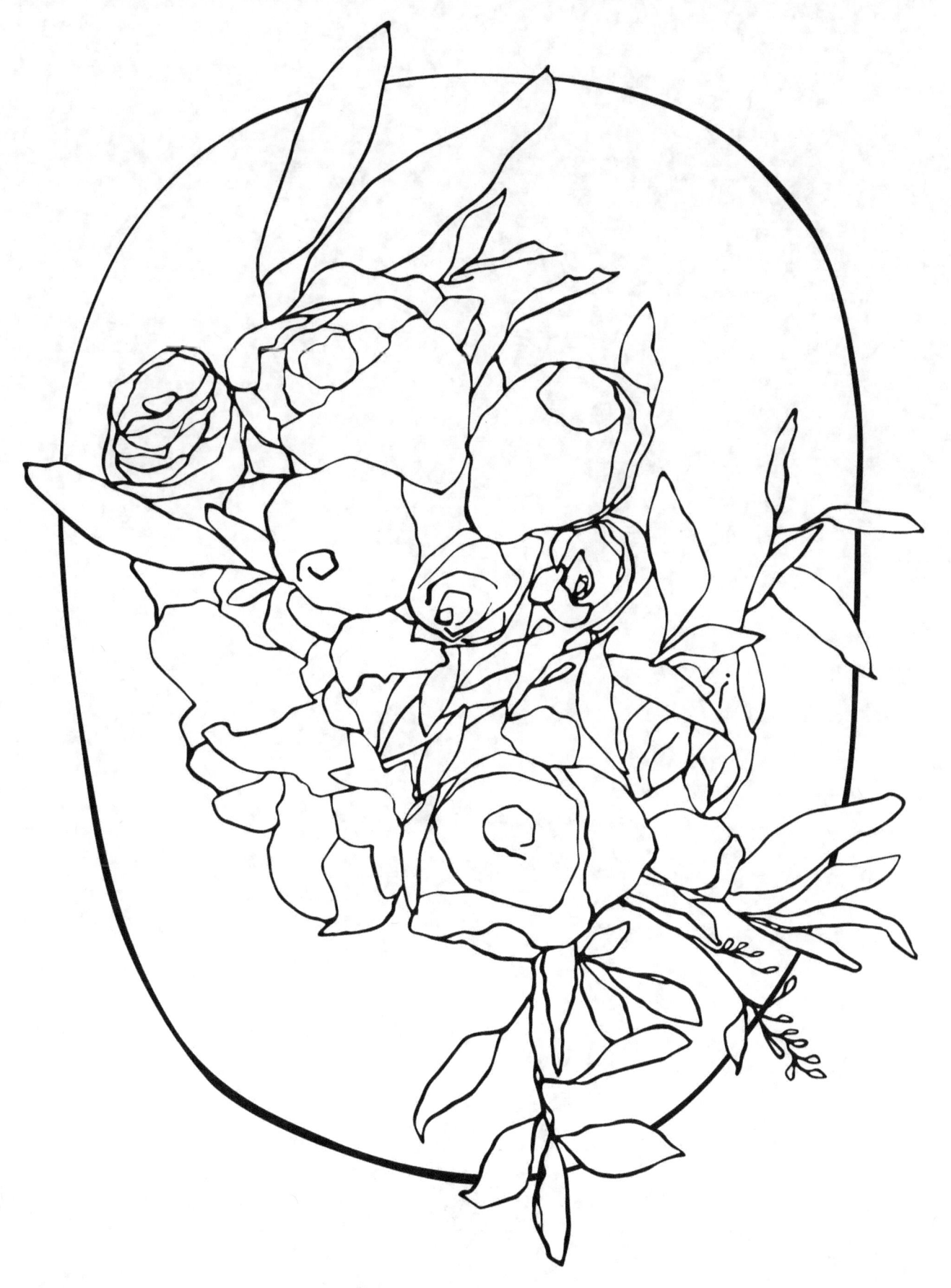

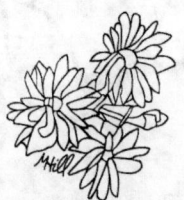

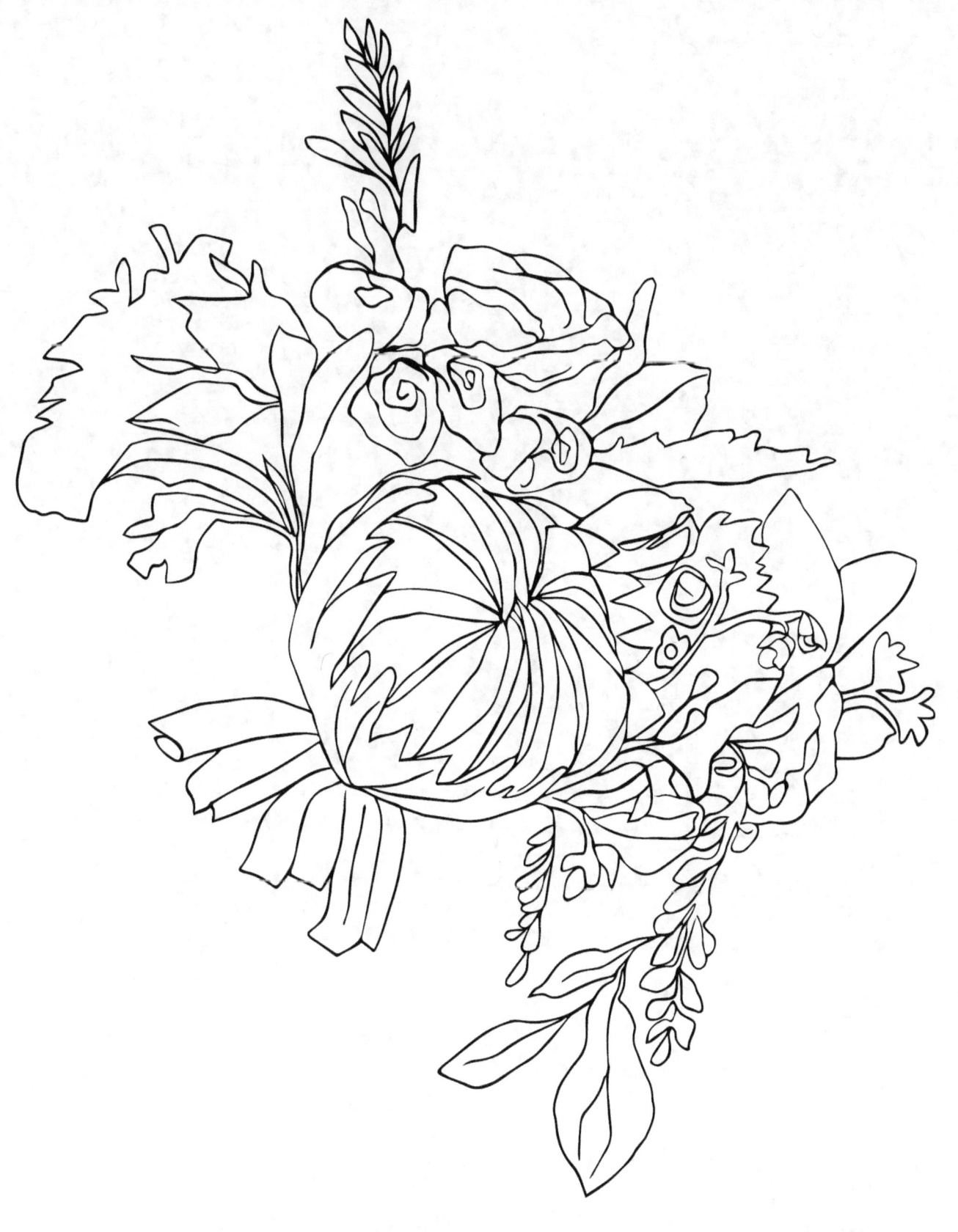

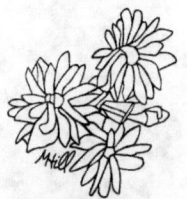

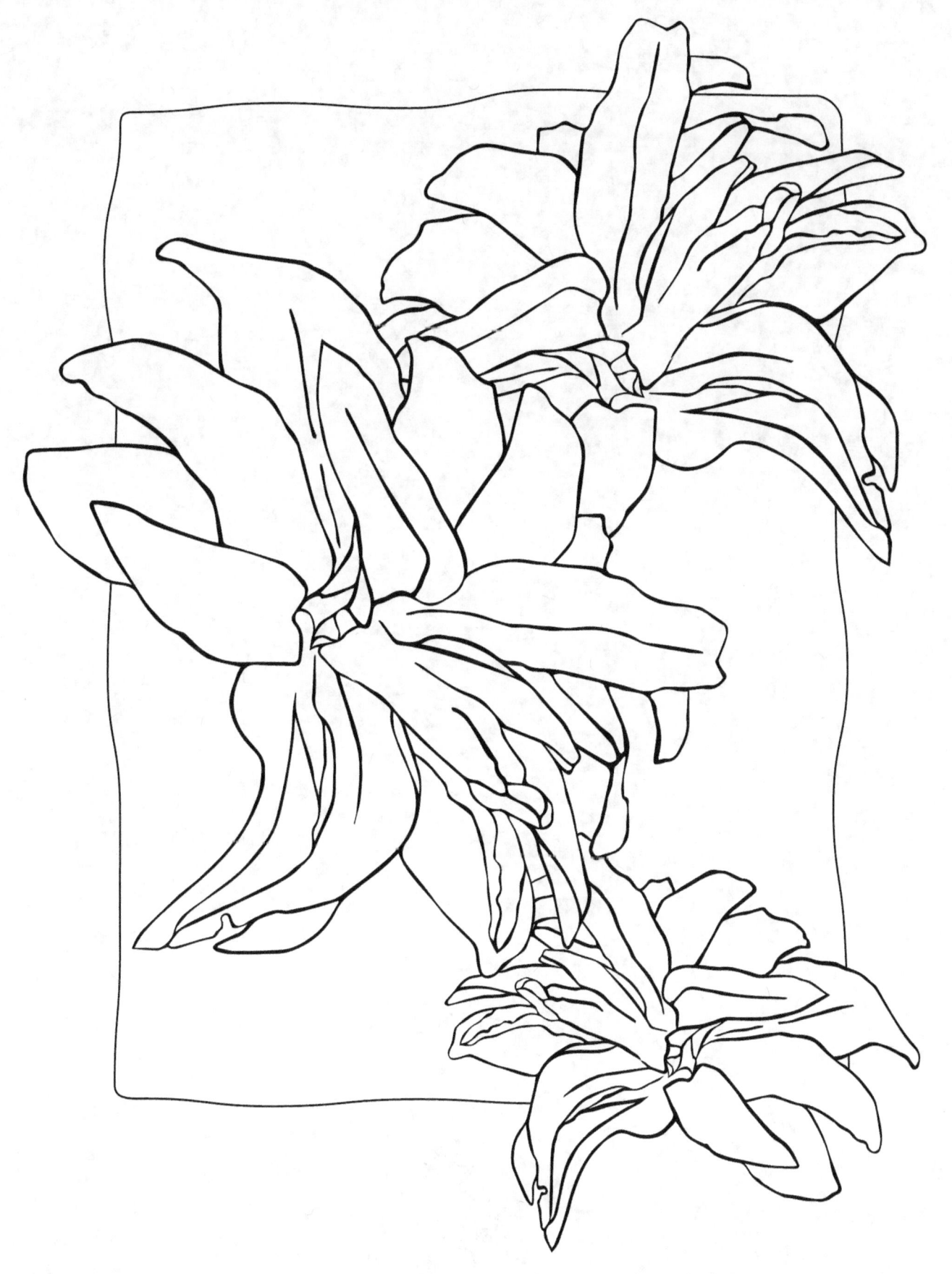

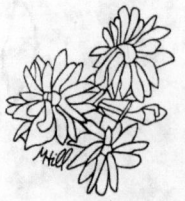

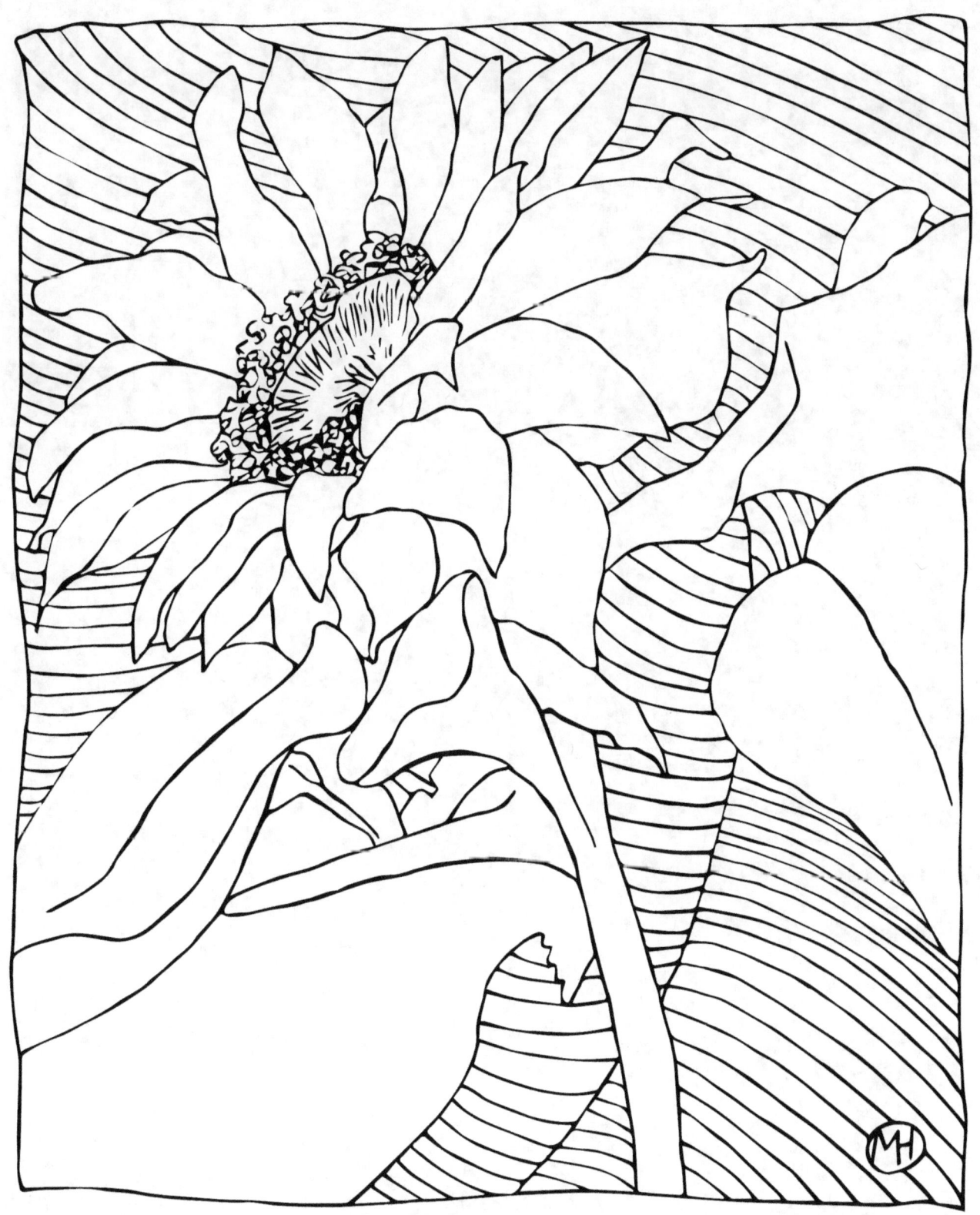

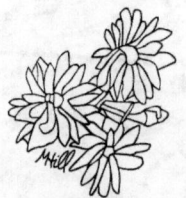

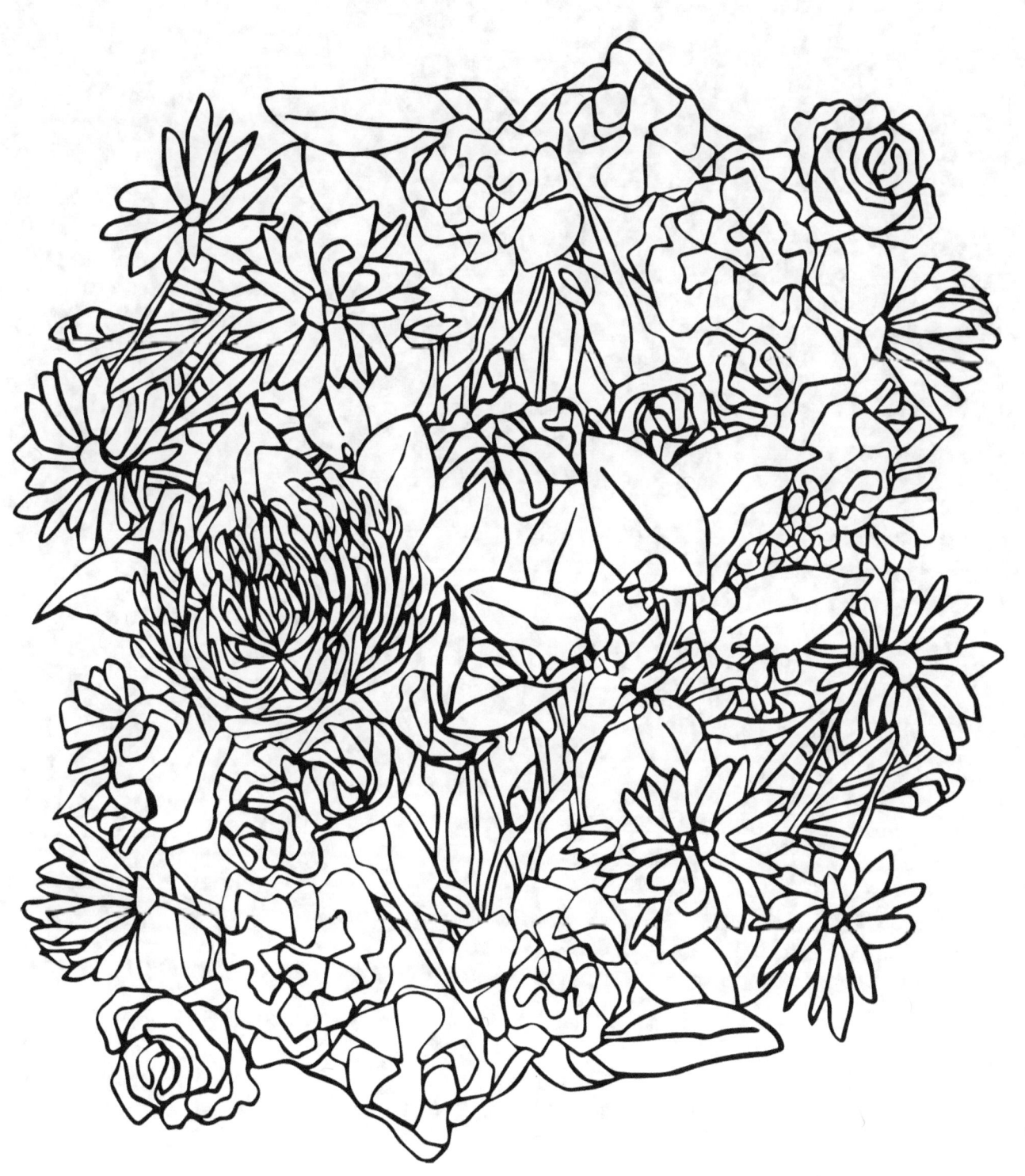

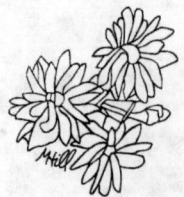

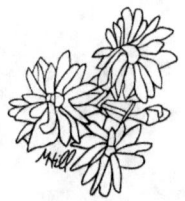